JANET SCHAEFFLER, OP

THE CATECHIST'S GUIDE TO BELOVED CATHOLIC PRAYERS

UNDERSTANDING AND SHARING THE TRADITION

TWENTY-THIRD PUBLICATIONS
twentythirdpublications.com

Twenty-Third Publications
One Montauk Avenue, Suite 200
New London, CT 06320
(860) 437-3012 or (800) 321-0411
www.twentythirdpublications.com

Cover photo: iStock.com / Ralf Geithe
Interior image: iStock.com / artisteer

ISBN: 978-1-62785-464-1
Library of Congress Control Number: 2019940115
Printed in the U.S.A.

bayard A division of Bayard, Inc.

CONTENTS

INTRODUCTION

"It is better to say one Our Father fervently and devoutly than a thousand with no devotion and full of distraction."

SAINT EDMUND (841–869)

St. Ignatius (1491–1556) once suggested to those who were searching to grow in prayer to pray the Our Father very slowly and silently in harmony with the pattern of deep, relaxed breathing. St. Ignatius also recommended a second method: become relaxed and dwell on the first word of the Our Father, for as long as it is meaningful. Then, move on to the second word.

A young novice once asked St. Teresa of Ávila (1515–1582), "Mother, what shall I do to become a contemplative?" Without missing a beat, Teresa responded, "Say the Our Father—but take an hour to say it."

In her autobiography, St. Thérèse of Lisieux (1873–1897), wrote that "Sometimes when I am in such a state of spiritual dryness that not a single good thought occurs to me, I say very slowly the 'Our Father,' or the 'Hail Mary,' and these prayers suffice to take me out of myself, and wonderfully refresh me."

During a homily at Saint Martha's House (a building adjacent to St. Peter's Basilica in Vatican City) on January 12, 2018, Pope Francis said that the gospel reading (which they had just heard) should prompt people to reflect on how they pray. Do people pray like "parrots," echoing words with no interest or care in what one is asking or do people "beg the Lord to help us (in) our little faith" and keep at it no matter the difficulties?

Our Catholic tradition has given us a rich treasury of prayers that enable us to pray as one community, for we all know, respect, and value the same words.

Once we memorize these prayers and deeply imprint them in our minds and hearts, however, how do we pray them? Are there times when we pray them on autopilot? Are there occasions when we pray them in parrot-like fashion? Do we know them so well that we don't really pray the words, pray the meaning, listen for the comfort, and become aware of the challenge?

The saints quoted above (and many others) and Pope Francis (and many other guides on our faith journey) have reminded us to pray these memorized prayers slowly, reflectively, and attentively, allowing the significance and implications of the words to enter our minds, hearts, and lives.

This book is a guide to ten of our cherished prayers. Much has been written—and could be written—on each of them. This is a short and introductory exploration of:

- Their history,
- Reflections on the words of the prayer,
- Suggested questions for prayerful reflection and conversations,
- Some additional ways to pray,
- Possible activities for home and/or faith formation use.

Even though we have named the book *A Catechist's Guide...*, many Christians—individually, in small groups, in families, or in adult faith formation opportunities—will find it encouraging and expanding for their own prayer lives.

Catechists (of children, youth, and adults) will discover some of the foundational realities and profound meanings of these treasured prayers—for themselves and to share with their learners. The suggested reflection questions will help catechists during their personal prayer and will provide conversation starters during catechetical gatherings. The best way to "learn" prayer, of course, is not just to read about it but to do it. As this book explores each of these ten prayers, further suggestions are provided to expand the praying (and living) of the meaning of each prayer. Practical recommendations are given for catechists to help learners experience the prayers during faith formation sessions and suggestions to send home to support and encourage family prayer.

G.K. Chesterton once said, "You say grace before meals. All right. But I say grace before the play and the opera, and grace before the concert and pantomime, and grace before I open a book, and grace before sketching, painting, swimming, fencing, boxing, walking, playing, dancing; And grace before I dip the pen in the ink." For Chesterton, prayer was all-encompassing; there wasn't an area of life that didn't call him to praise and thanksgiving, to a deeper awareness and connection with our ever-present, unconditionally loving God.

As you use this book to more deeply understand, love, and live these prayers of our Catholic community, may you more deeply experience our faithful God and share God's compassion with all those you touch.

The OUR FATHER

Our Father,
who art in heaven,
hallowed be thy name;
thy kingdom come,
thy will be done
on earth as it is in heaven.
Give us this day our daily bread,
and forgive us our trespasses,
as we forgive those who
  trespass against us;
and lead us not into temptation,
but deliver us from evil.
Amen.

HISTORY AND BACKGROUND

We have received the Our Father from three sources. The shortest, and perhaps closest to Jesus' words, is in the Gospel of Luke (11:1–4) when the disciples ask Jesus to teach them to pray. Matthew's longer version, in the sermon that includes the Beatitudes (6:9–13), is the basis of the traditional formula on which all Christians draw. The *Didache* (a brief, anonymous "Teaching of the Twelve Apostles" from the first or second century) adds to Matthew's text: "For yours are the power and the glory forever."

Jesus often spoke about prayer: pray with humility (the tax collector rather than the Pharisee); persist in prayer (the widow before the judge); forgive others before offering your gift at the altar. Then, Jesus gave his followers a prayer that reminds us of all these things (and much more). In the *Didache*, Christians were encouraged to pray the Lord's Prayer three times each day. Today the Our Father is a frequent daily prayer for many Christians; it is also an integral prayer at every liturgy, in the Liturgy of the Hours, in the Rosary, and in many other devotions and prayer times. The Our Father is not just a short prayer to memorize, not just nice words to fall back on. It is a comfort and a challenge; it is all-encompassing; it is foundational for our call as disciples.

A model for prayer

In Luke, the disciples did not say, "Give us a prayer" but "Teach us to pray." When Jesus shared these words, then, it was more than a simple prayer. It is a guide, a teaching story, a profound "handbook" about the attitudes needed for all prayer. Jesus gave us a pattern or model for prayer. He was teaching his disciples how to pray, how to approach God in all prayer: expressing adoration, recognizing

God's attributes, and petitions for the grace, needs, forgiveness, and protection needed by humankind—and praying all of this in a few sentences and in simple words. Most important, Jesus teaches us to pray based on his intimate relationship with God; he wants that relationship to be the basis for our prayer—and our lives.

A communal prayer

The *Catechism of the Catholic Church* (CCC) follows the Tridentine Catechism in emphasizing that the Our Father is a communal prayer. We, of course, pray it in community during our celebration of liturgy. Yet every time we pray it, we pray "*our* Father," not "*my* Father"; we pray "give *us* this day *our* daily bread," rather than "give *me*...." (CCC, 2789–2792). Even as we pray it individually, we pray as one people, as people of one family, God's inclusive family.

The content of the prayer

The *Catechism*, quoting St. Augustine, identifies seven petitions in the Our Father (CCC, 2803–2806). The first three focus on the glory of God, drawing us toward God for God's sake: God's name, the kingdom of God, and God's will. The last four center on requesting God's strength and help with our human needs and concerns.

The *Catechism* also quotes Tertullian, an early church father, who described the Lord's Prayer as, "truly the summary of the whole gospel" (CCC, 2761). Tertullian explained that the prayer incorporates, in concise form, "almost every word of the Lord, every remembrance of his teaching" (*On Prayer*, chapter 1).

REFLECTING ON THE WORDS OF THE PRAYER

Our

Nowhere in the Our Father do we find the words, "I," "me" or "mine." We begin the prayer with "Our" for two reasons: God is not only in relationship with Jesus, but with us; God is our father (Romans 8:15); and we are created as one, each of us is joined to everyone else for whom God is Creator and Father.

The *Catechism of the Catholic Church* stresses that the word *our* "excludes no one." The Our Father erases all boundaries; we are called into the universal family circle: saints and sinners, living and deceased, loved and feared, powerful and insignificant. "If we are to say it truthfully, our divisions and oppositions have to be overcome" (CCC, 2792).

Father,

Jesus could have chosen any title for God; many names for God are found in the Old Testament. By using "Father," Jesus was calling his followers to share in his deep and intimate and very special relationship with God. "Abba" was an intimate name, illustrating a relationship of concern, love, care, and ever-present availability.

Jesus was inviting us to do the same: to believe in the relationship that God desires, to experience the tender, nurturing, and secure presence of God. By using "father," Jesus' prayer was affirming that God intimately cares for us, rather than that stating that God is male. Father is an analogy, a valuable one, but an analogy, for we can only talk of the mystery of God through analogy, images, and metaphors.

Jesus invites us to pray—and live—in a radical relationship with God; we are intimate members of the family, welcome at the family table.

who art in heaven

When Jesus referred to heaven, he never spoke of a place but described a state of the heart, a way of being attentive to the sacred in ordinary things. The *Catechism* notes: "Who Art in Heaven: This biblical expression does not mean a place ('space'), but a way of being; it does not mean that God is distant, but majestic. Our Father is not 'elsewhere': he transcends everything we can conceive of his holiness" (CCC, 2794). This line in the prayer confirms that God is always present here and now—in the everydayness of our lives. Jesus compared heaven to small things: a mustard seed, a pearl of great price, a treasure hidden in a field—our hearts and attentiveness to all blessings connect us to the continual presence of God, heaven with us.

hallowed be thy name;

We can find echoes of this petition in the first three commandments, which affirm that God is one, holy, and sacred. We also find resonances in the words of Isaiah: "Holy, holy, holy is the Lord of hosts!" (6:3).

We, of course, do not make God's name holy, sanctified, and blessed; it already is. When we pray these words, we proclaim that God—the very essence of God—is holy. We are praying that we will always remember that.

This petition calls us to praise God; to honor God's name, which points to God's essential nature; to recognize God's presence and appreciate the gift of life, of grace. It is finding words for what God is doing in us and in our world today. Perhaps, too, it calls us—in our prayer—to not only ask for our needs but to first recognize God's holiness and goodness.

This petition also challenges us to an ever-growing holiness.

St. Peter Chrysologus, cited in the *Catechism of the Catholic Church*, said, "But we ask that this name of God should be hallowed in us through our actions. For God's name is blessed when we live well... We ask then that, just as the name of God is holy, so we may obtain his holiness in our souls" (CCC, 2814).

thy kingdom come,

The *Catechism of the Catholic Church* reminds us that our text of the Our Father is a translation; the Greek word we translate as "kingdom" can also be translated as "reign" (CCC, 2816). Many Scripture translations prefer "reign" because it better describes the belief that God's reign is a condition or action rather than a place, an earthly realm.

Jesus' teaching and mission focused on a central theme: the reign of God. The first words out of Jesus' mouth in Mark (a literary tip-off that this might be important) are, "The kingdom of God is at hand. Repent, and believe in the gospel" (1:15). In Luke 4:43: Jesus says: "To the other towns also I must proclaim the good news of the kingdom of God, because for this purpose I have been sent." Likewise, Jesus called his followers to make God's reign their first priority: "But seek first the kingdom of God and his righteousness, and all these things will be given you besides" (Matthew 6:33).

Living in the reign of God is a life of prayerfulness; a life of presence and of seeing God everywhere; a life of unconditional love of all people; a life of service, mercy, and justice; a life of communion with all God's people. We pray that we will be instruments of bringing about God's dream of loving goodness for all creation. We bring the reign of God when we go beyond ourselves in love, in hospitality, in justice, and weave into a compassionate community those among whom we live and work.

thy will be done
on earth as it is in heaven.

Scripture, of course, continually asserts for us God's will. This includes the commandments; the words of Micah 6:8 ("You have been told, O mortal, what is good, and what the Lord requires of you: Only to do justice and to love goodness, and to walk humbly with your God"), Jesus' two great commandments (Matthew 22:36–40; John 13:34) and our actions that mirror Jesus' role (Luke 4:16–19). Jesus continually teaches that we enter heaven not because of our words but by doing the will of God (Matthew 7:21; CCC, 2826).

As we pray this portion of the Our Father, we join Jesus in the Garden of Gethsemane and face the ongoing struggle and balance between our needs and expectations and God's bigger picture. Perhaps "thy will be done" is a litmus test for our faith, the trusting response because we acknowledge that our wise and loving God knows more than we do about what is best. Our first prayers often ask God for favors, explaining to God what we want to happen. Then our prayer changes to a willingness to receive what we are given, to find peace and healing in whatever happens because God is with us.

In the second portion of this line, we are offered an astonishing gift: we can live in heaven right here on earth. God's will is lived in heaven; when God's will is done on earth, earth will be like heaven. The reign of God is within us and among us; we are invited to live simply and kindly: to feed the hungry, to clothe the naked, to welcome the stranger. The Our Father challenges us to bring Jesus' vision of wholeness for humankind to our earth.

A focus on heaven does not mean giving up on this world. Sometimes our culture tells us that heaven and earth are opposites, that loving heaven can only mean we don't care about this world. Jesus' prayer is the opposite.

Give us this day our daily bread,

At first glance, this seems to be one of the simplest phrases of the Our Father, yet it is a petition that has many meanings and calls forth committed responsibility from each of us. Each word is filled with meaning and challenge.

We pray for more than bread; bread is a symbol of life's basics: our physical needs (food, water, shelter, clothing, education, healthcare) as well as our spiritual nourishment (hope, reassurance, comfort, peace of mind, strength). We pray for God's gifts that sustain our lives, all the things we need for our commitment about living like it's done in heaven. Since bread suggests healthy basic nourishment, this is a petition for what we need, not for all we desire or want (we don't pray for lobster or steak, expensive cars or luxurious vacations).

As we pray "give," we recognize that all we have is God's gift; therefore, thanksgiving needs to be our constant prayer.

We often pray the Our Father privately, but as we noted above, we never pray as individuals. The pronouns "us" and "our" assert that we are praying in communion with others and we are responsible for others; "us" and "our" makes this more than a petition—it commits us to responsibility for others. If I have enough, others should too. Our prayer also goes beyond words. It is not enough to pray that others have their daily needs met; we also need to work to make it happen. The *Catechism of the Catholic Church* teaches us that "The drama of hunger in the world calls Christians who pray sincerely to exercise responsibility toward their brethren....This petition...cannot be isolated from the parables of the poor man Lazarus and of the Last Judgment" (CCC, 2831).

We pray for bread one day at a time. In explaining the gift of manna to God's people, Moses said, "It is the bread the Lord has given you to eat. This is what the Lord has commanded: 'Everyone is to gather as much as they need'" (Exodus 16:15–16). For those who took more than they needed, by the next morning it bred worms and became smelly. This was a reminder that God would give them each day what they needed. Today, we acknowledge God's greatness, guidance, and generosity and pray with trust that God will provide for us each day.

and forgive us our trespasses,
as we forgive those who trespass against us;

In these lines we pray to do something. In the previous petitions we primarily ask *God* to do something (for instance, "let your kingdom come" rather than "God, I will make your kingdom come"). Even here, we first ask God to forgive us, but then we say what we will do.

Because of what we say we will do, this is perhaps the most challenging part of the prayer: to forgive again and again. We are acknowledging that God's forgiveness is not something we can keep to ourselves. If we have received this precious gift, we have no right to refuse it to another.

It is not a question of God withholding forgiveness, but rather that our unforgiving hearts make us unreceptive to God. "In refusing to forgive our brothers and sisters, our hearts are closed and their hardness makes them impervious to the Father's merciful love..." (CCC, 2840).

This petition is related to the rest of the Our Father: The kingdom (reign) is the kingdom of forgiveness. God's will is that we forgive. We honor God's name when we forgive. We bring heaven to earth when we forgive.

The call to forgiveness—which is pervasive in the gospels—

is not only on a personal level but pervades all relationships, all groups, and all our efforts. After 9/11, St. John Paul II titled his World Day of Peace proclamation for 2002, "No Peace without Justice; No Justice without Forgiveness." Reflecting on 9/11, as well as the enormous suffering of others throughout the world, St. John Paul said: "But because human justice is always fragile and imperfect, subject as it is to the limitations and egoism of individuals and groups, it must include and, as it were, be completed by the *forgiveness which heals and rebuilds troubled human relations from their foundations*. This is true in circumstances great and small, at the personal level or on a wider, even international scale. Forgiveness is in no way opposed to justice, as if to forgive meant to overlook the need to right the wrong done. It is rather the fullness of justice, leading to that tranquility of order which is much more than a fragile and temporary cessation of hostilities, involving as it does the deepest healing of the wounds which fester in human hearts. Justice and forgiveness are both essential to such healing" (3).

and lead us not into temptation,

This has often been called the problem petition; it has raised questions for some, giving the impression that God directly or intentionally causes temptation.

On December 6, 2017, Pope Francis mentioned that the current English translation is not a good one because God does not lead people to sin. Pope Francis suggested using "do not let us fall into temptation." He said, "It is not God who throws me into temptation and then sees how I fell...A father does not do that; a father helps you to get up immediately."

The apostle James reminds us, "No one experiencing temptation should say, 'I am being tempted by God'; for God is not subject to temptation to evil, and he himself tempts no one" (James 1:13). Some countries (e.g., Benin, France, Switzerland) are using wording that conveys "do not let us enter into temptation." Canada began using that wording in December 2018. Bishop André Gazaille of Nicolet, Québec, wrote that the new version "better reflects the spirit of the prayer taught by Jesus to his disciples." Many Scripture scholars point out that this phrase, found in the gospels of Matthew and Luke, can be translated literally by "let us not go in the direction of temptation."

In praying this line (in whatever translation), we are acknowledging the reality of temptation. In the midst of desiring God's will to be done, longing for God's reign, we also experience wanting our own will, craving for other things more than craving for God's reign. As we pray this petition, we are asking God for the gift of wisdom, the gift of discernment, the gift of God's strength to choose the good. We, once again, affirm our reliance on God, God's support and guidance for everything in our lives.

but deliver us from evil.
Amen.

"In this final petition," says the *Catechism*, "the Church brings before the Father all the distress of the world. Along with deliverance from the evils that overwhelm humanity, she implores the precious gift of peace and the grace of perseverance in expectation of Christ's return" (CCC, 2854).

This last petition, in some ways, is the most practical, expressing how we often experience life. How often do we pray (or think), "Please, God, just help me stay out of trouble; let nothing bad happen to my loved ones and to me"?

Similar to the previous petition, we are affirming confident dependence on God. We believe that our provident God will always help us.

For the kingdom, the power, and the glory
are yours, now and forever.

Found not in the gospels, but in some of the old liturgical books of Eastern rites and the *Didache* (a "catechism" of the first or second century), this doxology (a hymn of praise) was added to bring the Our Father full circle. It "takes up again, by inclusion, the first three petitions to our Father: the glorification of his name, the coming of his reign, and the power of his saving will. But these prayers are now proclaimed as adoration and thanksgiving, as in the liturgy of heaven" (*Catechism of the Catholic Church*, 2855).

In 1970 Pope Paul VI adapted and linked this ancient doxology with the praying of the Our Father during our celebration of the liturgy.

QUESTIONS FOR REFLECTION AND CONVERSATION

Which line of the prayer means most to you today? Why?

Are you satisfied with praying the Our Father the way you always have? Might there be new ways of praying it?

What two recent events have helped you realize that God's reign is in your life? Where do you see God's reign in the world today?

What are your favorite names for God? We are called to be like God. What do those names call you to be like?

What is God's will for you?

How does God give you daily bread?

Are there hurts you need to forgive and let go? Are there relationships you need to mend and restore?

Because you pray the Our Father, is God calling you to do something differently in your life?

IDEAS FOR CONTINUING PRAYER

- Imagine God, like a loving parent, holding you close, telling you how deeply you are loved. Relax in the embrace of your loving God.
- Choose one line of the Our Father. Write your own prayer, using that petition as your theme.
- As you reflect on "Thy will be done," pray the prayer of Fr. Mychal Judge (a Franciscan priest and chaplain to the New York City Fire Department who died during the 9/11 attacks on the World Trade Center): *Lord, take me where you want me to go, let me meet who you want me to meet, tell me what you want me to say, and keep me out of your way.*

- If you prayed "thy love be done" (instead of "thy will be done"), would that change anything for you?
- At the Church of Pater Noster in the Holy Land, Christians recall Christ's teaching the Lord's Prayer to his disciples. On the walls of the church, translations of the Lord's Prayer in 140 languages are inscribed on colorful plaques. Learn the Our Father in another language.
- Use "Thy kingdom come" as a prayer throughout the day, especially when you see someone bringing the reign of justice and peace to our world.

SUGGESTIONS FOR FAMILIES AND/OR CATECHETICAL SESSIONS

As a family—or class—compile a booklet on the Our Father, each page containing one phrase with matching pictures.

Be on the lookout for magazine/newspaper/internet articles and TV shows that are related to the lines of the Lord's Prayer.

Designate a week to use your cell phone camera to take pictures of situations that illustrate each line of the Our Father.

Design and make an Our Father quilt with each quilt block containing the words and illustration of one of the lines of the prayer.

Make a tablecloth for your dining room table or prayer table. Using fabric crayons, write the lines of the Our Father around the edges.

The HAIL MARY

Hail Mary, full of grace.
The Lord is with you.
Blessed are you among women,
and blessed is the fruit of your womb,
Jesus.
Holy Mary, Mother of God,
pray for us sinners,
now and at the hour of our death.
Amen.

HISTORY AND BACKGROUND

This well-known prayer to Mary consists of three sentences; two are Scriptural greetings (Luke 1:28 and Luke 1:42), and the third is a petition, a humble request for Mary to pray for us.

There is little or no trace of the Hail Mary as a devotional prayer before about 1050. Around that time, on Marian feasts, monastic orders were beginning to use the Little Office of Mary, a devotional prayer patterned on the Divine Office (the Liturgy of the Hours). This Office contained the words of Gabriel and Elizabeth from the Gospel of Luke in its verses and responses. Gradually it became a practice, not only for the monks but also for the laity, to use these sentences as a prayer. In the year 1196 the bishop of Paris directed his clergy to teach these words to their flocks (along with the Lord's Prayer and the Creed). Similar enactments became frequent in every part of the world, and within a short time the prayer became well known by Catholic people.

Elizabeth—in Scripture—does not include the name of Jesus in her greeting to Mary; it was probably added to the prayer by Pope Urban IV (1261–64).

The third sentence of the prayer came into use about the year 1500 because of the conviction that this prayerful devotion would be more comprehensive if, because Mary is our mother, it included our petition for her intercession.

REFLECTING ON THE WORDS OF THE PRAYER

Hail Mary, full of grace. The Lord is with you.

We begin the Hail Mary echoing the greeting of Gabriel to Mary in Luke's gospel, into which the church, in this prayer, has inserted her name. In the times of Mary and Joseph, "hail" was a greeting used for royal or noble persons.

Hail can also be translated as "rejoice." Over the grotto of the Annunciation in Nazareth, there is a depiction of Mary and Gabriel dancing with great joy. Gabriel understood the world-changing implications of God's message he was bringing to Mary. A modern-day fresco by Megan Marlatt depicts Gabriel upside down, with the words upside down and backward. Gabriel knew that this message was making Mary's world topsy-turvy, turning it upside down.

In two different ways, Gabriel assures Mary of God's presence with her. The literal meaning of grace is "God's life in us." Thus, if Mary is full of grace, God is deeply with her. The phrase "the Lord is with you" (or its near equivalent) occurs throughout Scripture, especially when people have been entrusted with a mission of far-reaching implications. Mary found the strength to answer yes because she was assured that she was not alone.

Blessed are you among women, and blessed is the fruit of your womb, Jesus.

Until the name "Jesus" in the prayer, these are the words that Mary's cousin Elizabeth speaks to her when Mary arrives to visit and help Elizabeth, who was pregnant with John the Baptist (Luke 1:42). The *Catechism of the Catholic Church* reminds us, too, that "Since that time, countless saints through the ages have called

Mary 'blessed.'...Mary is 'blessed among women' because she believed in the fulfillment of the Lord's word" (CCC, 2767).

As we pray, we recognize—along with Elizabeth—that Mary is the mother of our Lord.

Holy Mary, Mother of God, pray for us sinners, now and at the hour of our death. Amen.

This third part of the prayer reflects the church's belief in Mary's role as the Mother of God. Mary, as one of us, as our mother, also has a preeminent place in the communion of saints, interceding for all God's people.

At times, people question why we pray to Mary. Are we placing her before God? During our lives, we often ask others to pray with and for us. This also occurred in Scripture. St. Paul says, "you help us by your prayers" (2 Corinthians 1:11). St. James says, "pray for one another" (James 5:16).

St. Paul and St. James are talking about the faithful on earth. Our belief in the communion of saints guides us to an inclusive reality of how God made us—we are all and always interconnected. Those on earth and those who have gone before us are all one family. When we die, we do not leave this family.

We ask one another to pray for us here on earth (when we're going through a hard time, at times of illness or discouragement, etc.). Since Mary is fully alive in heaven and is integrally connected with us, she, too, can be asked to pray with and for us.

"At the hour of our death" calls to mind Mary's presence with Jesus at the foot of the cross; knowing Mary was with him (and probably Joseph at his death), with trust we pray for Mary's intercession at the time of our death. Perhaps, too, we are asking for Mary's prayers in all of our "deaths"—our daily fears, problems, struggles, and griefs as well as the constant journey of dying to self, our weaknesses, our faults, and our selfishness.

QUESTIONS FOR REFLECTION AND CONVERSATION

We pray: "full **of** *grace..." What are you full of? What are you made of?*

God—in various ways—sends us, too, the message "the Lord is with you." When you really think about that message, how do you feel? When do you most experience God's presence with you?

We pray: "pray for **us***" not "pray for* **me***." Why do you think this is the word (us) the church uses? Whom do you pray for? Do you leave anyone out?*

We pray: "pray...now..." Are there times you think "I'll have time later to pray, to listen, to take time for God, for others, later, when I'm not so busy"? What is it time for you to do ***now****?*

IDEAS FOR CONTINUING PRAYER

- The Hail Mary and the Latin, *Ave Maria*, have been the inspiration for many musical settings, for instance: https://www.youtube.com/watch?v=REROQ1biLdE. Use one of these renditions or put the words to your own music.
- In this prayer we call Mary "full of grace," "holy," and "Mother of God." Throughout the centuries, numerous titles and names have been given to Mary. As you recall and/or research them, which is your favorite? Why? Can you discover one you've never been aware of before? Which one(s) do you want to use in your prayer?
- The repetition of the Hail Mary in the Rosary is meant to lead us into meditative prayer focusing on each mystery. The gentle repetition of the prayer helps us to enter into the silence of our hearts, where God always lives. Pray the Rosary (or one decade) slowly, contemplatively.

SUGGESTIONS FOR FAMILIES AND/OR CATECHETICAL SESSIONS

Praying with gestures helps us to pray in two ways: with words and with actions. Think of gestures you might use for each phrase of the Hail Mary, e.g., *full of grace*: arms open wide; *Jesus*: head bowed; *pray for us sinners*: hands folded in prayer.

As you pray on different days, insert a different family member's (or children's) name: "Holy Mary, Mother of God, pray for _______, now and at the hour of (her or his) death."

Explore with children some of the various paintings that depict the Annunciation. What does each tell us about Mary, about God's message to her?

The GLORY BE

Glory be to the Father,
And to the Son,
And to the Holy Spirit.
As it was in the beginning,
is now,
and will be forever. Amen.

HISTORY AND BACKGROUND

The Glory Be is a prayer of faith—in essence the simplest and most essential creed, taking us to the heart of Christianity: God is revealed to us in three persons—the Father, Christ the Son, and the Holy Spirit.

This short prayer is prayed at various times: at the end of each decade of the Rosary, at the end of the psalms in the Liturgy of the Hours, to end a longer prayer, and, of course, as a prayer itself.

The Glory Be is also known as a doxology. A doxology is a short prayer of praise to God (*doxa* is the Greek word for glory) that can be spoken or sung in the form of a hymn. The Glory Be is often referred to as the Little Doxology; the Great Doxology is the *Gloria in Excelsis Deo*, the song of the angels in Luke 2:14 (which we pray during liturgy).

The tradition of the doxology comes from the Jewish synagogues. St. Paul often concluded his letters with doxologies similar to the Glory Be ("For of him, and by him, and in him, are all things: to him be glory for ever. Amen." [Romans 11:36])

As early as the year 300, Christians began using the phrase, "Glory be to the Father, and to the Son, and to the Holy Spirit" to give praise to God and to promote belief in the Trinity.

Throughout the fourth century, as a reminder to the faithful to continually turn toward God, the church encouraged the frequent repetition of the Glory Be by adding it to each psalm. Later, as the Rosary became a favored devotion, the Glory Be was added to the conclusion of each decade.

Throughout the ages, various forms of the Glory Be have been fervently prayed. In 1608 St. Francis de Sales ended his classic book *Introduction to the Devout Life*: "Glory be to Jesus, to Whom, with the Father and the Holy Ghost, be honor and glory, now and ever, and to all Eternity. Amen."

REFLECTING ON THE WORDS OF THE PRAYER

Glory be to the Father,
And to the Son,
And to the Holy Spirit.

"Glory" is the translation of a Hebrew word for majesty, even heaviness. God is the weighty one, the constant one, the significant one. Even if everything else disappeared, God would remain.

"Glory" calls us to ponder the majesty, the awesomeness, of God. The word takes us beyond the ordinary, reminding us that there is beauty and generosity that is beyond our imagining.

As a profession of faith, the Glory Be follows the baptismal formula found in Matthew 28:19 ("baptizing them in the name of the Father, and of the Son, and of the holy Spirit"), clearly communicating the equality of the persons of the Trinity. In the early centuries of the church, several heresies were espoused rejecting the equality of the Trinity. This early prayer was a rejection of these heresies. Perhaps the important word is "and"; not only do we say that the Trinitarian God has glory, but we also profess that each member of the Trinity shares equally in that glory.

The message of our faith is that the glory of God has come among us: Jesus who walked among us shares in the glory of the Father and the Holy Spirit.

As it was in the beginning,
is now,
And will be forever. Amen.

This second part of the prayer professes that God is everlasting. The Father, Son, and Holy Spirit were one from the beginning of time and will continue to be forever. In the early heresies, some had asserted that the Son had not always existed, thereby denying the eternity of the Trinity.

In this short sentence we bring together all of time (which God sees and lives differently than our humanity can understand and experience): the *beginning* (not "beginning" as we understand it, for "Your throne stands firm from of old; you are from everlasting" [Psalm 93:2]); the *present*; and the *future* (which never ends). We affirm: the beginning, which wasn't a starting; every moment along the way; and forever and ever (without any ending)!

Often we hear and pray the ending sentence in this way: "As it was in the beginning is now, and ever shall be, world without end." The ending Latin words for this sentence, "*saecula saeculorum*," literally mean "time of times," which would then translate as "forever and ever." The challenge is that "*saecula*" has a range of meanings: generation, average human life span, century. Because of recent enhanced understandings of Latin, Greek, and Hebrew, the church, in the late 1960s, changed the traditional wording to: "is now and will be forever." The older translation is still often used in private prayer; this revised version is always prayed in the public prayer of the church, especially in the Liturgy of the Hours.

QUESTIONS FOR REFLECTION AND CONVERSATION

The Glory Be has been prayed by our ancestors in the faith. When you pray it, who are the people who have lived before you that you imagine are still now praying it with you?

In your prayer, whom do you usually pray to—the Father, Son, or Holy Spirit?

What would it mean for your life—for your prayer and for your actions—to believe that the glory of God was being poured into you?

IDEAS FOR CONTINUING PRAYER

- Pray your own prayer of praise: tell God of your love; give thanks for who God is and what God has done for you; sing songs of praise, etc.
- The Glory Be affirms the eternal glory of "God in Three Persons, Blessed Trinity," as God is named in the well-known hymn "Holy, Holy, Holy." Find the hymn (on YouTube) to use in morning prayer.
- On your busy days, could a "Glory Be" provide a pause once in a while to recall God's love for you?
- Pray the prayer with long pauses between phrases: Glory... to the Father...to the Son..., etc. Reflect on what you are really saying in these words. What insights, what feelings, what gratitude surfaces for you?

SUGGESTIONS FOR FAMILIES AND/OR CATECHETICAL SESSIONS

Decide on a certain time of the day. Wherever you are (school, home, work, at play) stop and pray the Glory Be, knowing that your family (your classmates) are praying with you.

As you read the Glory Be and the Gloria, write your own prayer of praise to God the Father, Son, and Holy Spirit.

Decide on simple gestures to use in praying the Glory Be.

At times, pray together the Glory to God hymn from our liturgy.

PRAYER *to the* HOLY SPIRIT

Come, Holy Spirit, fill the hearts
of your faithful and kindle in them
the fire of your love.

V. Send forth your Spirit, and they
shall be created.
R. And you shall renew the face of the earth.

O, God, who by the light of the Holy Spirit,
did instruct the hearts of the faithful, grant
that by the same Holy Spirit we may be
truly wise and ever enjoy his consolations.
Through Christ Our Lord. Amen.

HISTORY AND BACKGROUND

This ancient prayer is an example of how a popular prayer to the Holy Spirit was composed by the faithful, using verses they heard and prayed, especially at Pentecost.

We hear, "Come, Holy Spirit, fill the hearts of your faithful and kindle in them the fire of your love" with the allelluia before the gospel on Pentecost. It is also the antiphon for the *Magnificat* during the church's evening prayer.

The verse and response lines are taken from Psalm 104:30, describing God's sending forth the Spirit as God creates. "Send forth your spirit, they are created and you renew the face of the earth." This verse is the response in the responsorial psalm for Pentecost Sunday.

The rest of the prayer, asking for wisdom, has ancient liturgical roots. It can be found in the Gregorian Sacramentary, a liturgical book with prayers dating back to the ninth century or earlier. Today, it is also prayed as the opening prayer of the votive Mass of the Holy Spirit (sometimes used at the beginning of the school year.)

As Catholics pray this prayer today, praying with the early church and our ancestors throughout the ages, as well as joining with the prayers of Israel (the psalms), we pray for the continuing inspiration and guidance of the Holy Spirit.

REFLECTING ON THE WORDS OF THE PRAYER

Come, Holy Spirit, fill the hearts of your faithful and kindle in them the fire of your love.

The very last prayer in Scripture is "Come, Lord Jesus," the words of John in the Book of Revelation. Here we pray, "Come, Holy Spirit." Short prayers, but powerful.

Sometimes when we pray, "Come," we mean "please come and fix this problem, this challenge." We have in mind what we want the Holy Spirit to do for us; we know what we need. Our prayer is about us.

Perhaps this prayer is more about our realization that we know that the Holy Spirit is with us. We are recognizing that we feel something missing without the Holy Spirit in our lives. We are praying that we will be open to the Spirit's coming, the Spirit's presence. We are acknowledging that God knows what we need better than we do. We desire that the coming of the Spirit—the constant presence of the Spirit—change us; the Holy Spirit doesn't leave us the same as before we prayed. This is a bold petition. We're not praying for a little bit of the Holy Spirit. We are asking that we might be filled, completely, totally, entirely, with the strength, love, and vitality of the Spirit.

In fact, we not only ask for the Spirit's love but for the *fire* of the Spirit's love. We ask for a love that is powerful, that consumes, that changes and transforms. Tongues of fire (Acts 2:3) enlightened, strengthened, and empowered the disciples. We ask for the same kind of love so that our hearts may be on fire, and so that we may care more ardently, serve more creatively, give more lavishly, and love more extravagantly.

Send forth your Spirit, and they shall be created.
And you shall renew the face of the earth.

These lines—from Psalm 104 praising God for all creation—remind us that God is active in creating, in sustaining, and in recreating. By the Spirit, God creates and recreates.

Remembering Paul's words in 2 Corinthians 5:17—"So whoever is in Christ is a new creation: the old things have passed away; behold, new things have come"—we are asking the Spirit to make us a new creation. We are requesting more than a fresh start; we are praying for a deepened transformation.

When we are on fire through the Spirit, we can become one with the Spirit's work of renewing the world. We can be the fire that ignites other sparks and flames, and which brings healing, justice, and rebirth for all people, for all creation.

Let us pray.
O, God, who by the light of the Holy Spirit, did instruct the hearts of the faithful, grant that by the same Holy Spirit we may be truly wise and ever enjoy his consolations.
Through Christ Our Lord. Amen.

The first two parts of the prayer might be seen as a preparation for this closing prayer, a prayer *to* God *through* Christ *inspired by* the Holy Spirit. Recalling God's work in the people of the past, we pray that that same work continue today in us: that the Spirit guide us to be truly wise and to enjoy, that is, be consoled by, the gifts of the Spirit.

QUESTIONS FOR REFLECTION AND CONVERSATION

Do you remember a time when you said to yourself, "This is the Holy Spirit at work"? What was happening? What made you think it was the Holy Spirit's work?

Is there a particular area in your life where you rely on the presence of God's Spirit? How do you know that this is the Holy Spirit at work within you?

Have you ever experienced a "conversion," a "transformation"? To what or whom do you attribute this experience?

What life experience have you had that you think was influenced by the presence of the Holy Spirit?

Which title of the Holy Spirit do you most resonate with (some of the Spirit's titles: Comforter, Intercessor, Breath of God, Gentle Guest and Friend, Spirit of Unity)?

Which gift of the Holy Spirit (wisdom, knowledge, understanding, counsel, fortitude, piety, fear of the Lord) do you use most frequently? Which one do you want to deepen in your life right now?

IDEAS FOR CONTINUING PRAYER

- Wake up each morning with "Come, Holy Spirit" being the first words you say.
- Pray with the words of St. Augustine, a bishop from the fourth century.

  Breathe in me, O Holy Spirit,
  That my thoughts may all be holy.
  Act in me, O Holy Spirit,
  That my work, too, may be holy.
  Draw my heart, O Holy Spirit,
  That I love but what is holy.
  Strengthen me, O Holy Spirit,
  To defend all that is holy.
  Guard me, then, O Holy Spirit,
  That I always may be holy.

- Read the Acts of the Apostles. Be attentive to the presence and workings of the Holy Spirit in the early Christians, asking that you be open to the Spirit's guidance in your life.

SUGGESTIONS FOR FAMILIES AND/OR CATECHETICAL SESSIONS

Make a family prayer bulletin board. Cut out newspaper/magazine articles about people/situations that need the presence, power, and strength of the Holy Spirit. Include these in your family prayer. You might want to identify which fruit or gift of the Holy Spirit is needed in these situations.

On Pentecost (or any Sunday to celebrate the Spirit's life in your family), have a cake with white frosting. Place a circle of whole strawberries on top to represent the tongues of flame on the apostles' heads on the first Pentecost.

Periodically spend time (bedtime is an excellent time) so that mom and/or dad can tell each child which gift of the Spirit they see alive in him/her. Then the child(ren) can tell mom and/or dad the goodness he/she has seen in their parent(s) recently.

During dinner or while in the car, invite one another to share their thoughts and feelings about the following:

- If the Holy Spirit were a color, I think the Spirit would be ________.
- Scripture uses the symbols/images of fire, wind, breath, and dove for the Spirit. Invent a new one. What image or symbol says something about the Spirit for you?
- If the Spirit had three wishes for the world today, I think they would be ________.
- What advertising slogan would be a good description of the Holy Spirit?
- What does the Holy Spirit's touch feel like to you? How can you help the Holy Spirit touch our world?
- How would you describe the Holy Spirit to someone who has never heard of the Spirit?

GRACE *before* MEALS

Bless us, O Lord, and these your gifts
which we are about to receive
  from your goodness.
Through Christ our Lord.
Amen.

HISTORY AND BACKGROUND

We title this prayer "grace." We talk about "saying grace before meals." Grace comes from the Latin phrase *gratiarum action*, an act of thanks. Saying grace means giving thanks, remembering that we are not self-sufficient, and that it was God (and the work of others) that provided the gift of food. Should this be: that it is God (and the work of others) who *provides*.... (present tense rather than past)?

Praying before meals has deep roots in Scripture. God's people gave thanks for the manna that fell from heaven, sustaining them for forty years of wandering in the wilderness.

Deuteronomy 8:10 tells us, "But when you have eaten and are satisfied, you must bless the Lord, your God, for the good land he has given you." Early Christians, Jews, and Muslims all had prayers for before and/or after the meal, recalling a time when each morsel of food had to be hunted, gathered, or cultivated by hand. Gratitude was palpable because they knew each meal could be the last.

In Matthew's accounts of Jesus feeding thousands of people, before Jesus "broke the bread" (started the meal), he gave thanks to God. In Luke's account of the Last Supper, Jesus says, "he took a cup, gave thanks..." (Luke 22:20). When Luke recounts the Emmaus story, Jesus "took bread, said the blessing, broke it, and gave it to them" (Luke 24:30). Acts tells us that Paul "took bread, gave thanks to God in front of them all, broke it, and began to eat" (Acts 27:35).

Several early church fathers named the need to pray before meals. For example, Tertullian (in the early third century) noted in his treatise "On Prayer" that "it becomes believers not to take food...before interposing a prayer; for the refreshments and nourishments of the spirit are to be held prior to those of the flesh, and things heavenly prior to things earthly" (chapter 25).

The grace we pray today dates back to the Gelasian Sacramentary (the book of the church's liturgical prayer), which was compiled in the seventh or eighth century.

We pray grace before meals to ask God's blessings on those present and on the food we are about to eat. Does saying grace change things? In the movie *Shadowlands*, C.S. Lewis says that we pray because "the need flows out of me all the time—waking and sleeping. It doesn't change God—it changes me."

Grace before meals can be exactly that—a pause in our day, an act of trust in God's constant goodness to us. It is a time to slow down, to be aware and grateful for another day, another meal with nutritious food, and loved ones with whom to share.

REFLECTING ON THE WORDS OF THE PRAYER

Bless us, O Lord, and these your gifts

St. Paul reminds us that, because everything is a gift from God, it is appropriate to give "thanks always and for everything in the name of our Lord Jesus Christ to God the Father" (Ephesians 5:20). Thus, we give thanks for every meal—for the gifts of the earth, for the people who worked—in so many ways—that we might taste and enjoy.

As we pray before eating, we are expressing how much we need God's care—for the food itself and for how it brings us health, well-being, and connection with those with whom we share meals.

which we are about to receive from your goodness.

Many of us are familiar with praying "from thy bounty." "Bounty"—something that is given generously—is, of course, a word that is still used today, especially in referring to the fruits of the harvest. The Prayer Before Meals contained in the *Book of Blessings* (from the International Committee on English in the Liturgy, 1988), uses the more modern word "goodness." The meaning—using either word—of course, is a reminder to us that all that we have comes from our generous God.

Through Christ our Lord.
Amen.

We conclude this short blessing prayer as we end many of our prayers: through Christ. Often in Scripture Jesus tells us to pray in his name: "whatever you ask the Father in my name he will give you" (John 16:23). Paul reiterates this as he explains Jesus' ongoing priestly activity: "He is always able to save those who approach God through him, since he lives forever to make intercession for them" (Hebrews 7:25).

This ending also reminds us of another reason we pray this grace: we want Christ to be with us while we eat. What if we prayed before meals not because it's a ritual but because we're asking God to be with us during our meals? Jesus is always with us as he promised (Matthew 28:20). If we forget to pray, Jesus is still there. In praying, though, we remind ourselves of this presence, which is more constant, more intimate, than we can even imagine. We don't want an hour to pass or a meal to go by where we aren't aware of God with us. Taking moments of prayer—before meals, throughout the day's activities—helps us to continually deepen our attentiveness to how close God is.

QUESTIONS FOR REFLECTION AND CONVERSATION

Are there any times or places where you are embarrassed or hesitant to pray before meals?

When you pray a spontaneous grace, what petitions and gratitude do you include?

Does your grace before meals lead you to do anything after your meal?

In his encyclical Laudato Si', *Pope Francis encourages us to return to the "beautiful and meaningful custom" of prayer before and after meals: "That moment of blessing, however brief, reminds us of our dependence on God for life; it strengthens our feeling of gratitude for the gifts of creation; it acknowledges those who by their labors provide us with these goods; and it reaffirms our solidarity with those in greatest need" (227). Pope Francis names various reasons/results of grace before meals. Why do you pray before your meals?*

IDEAS FOR CONTINUING PRAYER

- Sing your grace—put a tune to our traditional prayer or write words to an existing tune.
- Paul encourages us to "give thanks in all circumstances" (1 Thessalonians 5:18). Give thanks for your basket of food when you're waiting in line at the grocery store, when you drive by farms, when you're enjoying a candy bar (or your favorite snack).
- Pray before meals in restaurants.
- Imagine eating in Jesus' presence. Imitate the way he eats. Which is he more focused on: his relationships or the food?
- Search for meal prayers from other cultures. You might want to download: https://www.yesmagazine.org/pdf/49/Graces_Poster11x17.pdf

SUGGESTIONS FOR FAMILIES AND/OR CATECHETICAL SESSIONS

Write a prayer before meals for different circumstances: for the drive-thru, to remember the Last Supper, for dining out, when someone is missing, to remember the hungry, for breakfast (lunch, dinner), for birthday celebrations.

Make placemats with various prayers before meals on them.

Collect various prayers before meals. Write them on small pieces of paper and place them in a box kept on your dinner table. Each night take out a different one.

During meal times, place your phones and other electronic devices in another room.

Plan a different focus for your meal prayers for various seasons of the year. For instance, during the month of November, name a family member or friend (or a person in the news) who has died, sharing a special memory of that person.

The ACT *of* CONTRITION

My God,
I am sorry for my sins with all my heart.
In choosing to do wrong
and failing to do good,
I have sinned against you
whom I should love above all things.
I firmly intend, with your help,
to do penance,
to sin no more,
and to avoid whatever leads me to sin.
Our Savior Jesus Christ
suffered and died for us.
In his name, my God, have mercy.

HISTORY AND BACKGROUND

An act of contrition can be a broad term for many prayers of sorrow within our tradition: the *Confiteor*, the Penitential Psalms (6, 32, 38, 51, 102, 130, 143), and the Gradual Psalms (119–133).

Usually when we talk about the Act of Contrition we are referring to the prayer prayed during the sacrament of reconciliation, before the priest gives a penance and prays the words of absolution. Many people also pray the act of contrition each evening.

Throughout the years there have been slightly different versions of the prayer. Throughout the nineteenth century and first half of the twentieth century, the most common form of the prayer was: "O my God I am heartily sorry for having offended thee, and I detest all my sins, because I dread the loss of heaven, and the pains of hell; but most of all because I love thee, my God, who art all good and deserving of all my love. I firmly resolve, with the help of thy grace, to confess my sins, to do penance, and to amend my life. Amen." The form we are using in this chapter is found in the *Rite of Penance*, 1974, and is the form commonly used today.

These various forms of the prayer have never been merely a magical formula said quickly to guarantee instant forgiveness. Rather, the prayer expresses in words an act that involves our desire and our promise. The words lead us to action through three necessary steps: an acknowledgment of doing wrong, an expression of sorrow, and a promise to change one's life and avoid sin.

In reality, the Act of Contrition is much more than a set prayer. It is at the center of our Catholic life, which began at our baptism. When our parents and godparents—on our behalf—renounced sin, they affirmed a way of life of grace, a way of life of goodness, a way of life of conversion.

REFLECTING ON THE WORDS OF THE PRAYER

My God,
I am sorry for my sins with all my heart.
In choosing to do wrong
and failing to do good,
I have sinned against you
whom I should love above all things.

The *Catechism of the Catholic Church* reminds us: "Among the penitent's acts contrition occupies first place. Contrition is sorrow of the soul and detestation for the sin committed, together with the resolution not to sin again" (CCC, 1451).

We are sorry "with all our heart" because "the desire for God is written in the human heart, because [the human being] is created by God and for God..." (CCC, 27). Our response to God—because of our failings—is not peripheral but is rooted in who we are, rooted in our intimate relationship with God.

Our sorrow is more than *feeling* sorrow; it is *being* sorry. The essence of being sorry is the regret or hatred for what we have done, accompanied by the firm determination, with God's help, of not doing it again.

We know that our sin hurts others, affects others, in countless ways. At the same time, sin disrupts God's generosity, God's design for us. God created us with unconditional love, sharing with us abundant gifts. God desires that we live in that love—with the Trinity and with all God's family.

I firmly intend, with your help,
to do penance,

In our sorrow, we regret the harm we have caused, and that leads us to do something: for our healing and the healing of those we have hurt. In the sacrament of reconciliation, the priest gives us a penance (for example, prayer, fasting, almsgiving, spiritual or corporal works of mercy, or service of neighbor) as a way to overcome selfishness and to recommit to live a holy life even more intensely. In the Act of Contrition, we promise to voluntarily do penance to be closer to God and to show to others the love and compassion of Jesus.

to sin no more,
and to avoid whatever leads me to sin.

The sincerity of our sorrow is illustrated by our resolve not to sin again. We express here our promise to do that, after first acknowledging that we need God's grace to live our promise.

We might think it's not possible to make this promise, for our faults and failings can be embedded in our lives. Our promise is the honest intention to make a serious, sustained effort not to sin again. Rather than thinking, "I'm sorry, but it's okay if I commit the sins again because I'll just go to confession," our promise in the Act of Contrition is: "I will do whatever I can not to commit these sins again. Even though I know I might fall back into my sin, I don't want to do that. I will try my best not to do that."

Our promise includes a determined effort to avoid any person, place, thing, or circumstance that could lead us into sin.

Our Savior Jesus Christ
suffered and died for us.
In his name, my God, have mercy.

God is pure mercy. Mercy is not just a characteristic that God has; it is *who* God is. Our prayer ends in a confident plea because God is unconditional love, total forgiveness, unending mercy.

QUESTIONS FOR REFLECTION AND CONVERSATION

When have you deeply experienced the forgiveness of another, of God?

As you think about your sin, your predominant fault(s), is it the same as it was ten years ago, twenty-five years ago? If yes, what might that say about your promise to work on changing your life?

Are there things that stand in your way of being truly sorry?

Is there an often-occurring attitude or action that stops you from being your best self?

IDEAS FOR CONTINUING PRAYER

- End each day with the Examen prayer: Become aware of God's presence. Give thanks for the gifts and blessings of the day. Pray that the Holy Spirit guide you as you look at your actions, attitudes, and motives. Review the day, recognizing any shortcomings and failures. Plan and pray about how you want to live tomorrow.
- Close each day with a prayerful reflection: Did I say only kind words today? Did I remember that my thoughts become my life? When did I see God? When did I give thanks today?
- End your day with Henri Nouwen's questions:

  Did I offer peace today?
  Did I bring a smile to someone's face?
  Did I say words of healing?
  Did I let go of my anger and resentment?
  Did I forgive?
  Did I love?

SUGGESTIONS FOR FAMILIES AND/OR CATECHETICAL SESSIONS

Write an act of contrition, being sure to include the three elements of contrition: an acknowledgment of doing wrong, an expression of sorrow, and a promise to change one's life and avoid sin.

Close your day with an examination of conscience for the day just lived together. Where did you bring love? When did you miss a chance to bring love?

The MEMORARE

Remember, O most gracious Virgin Mary,
that never was it known that anyone
who fled to your protection, implored
your help, or sought your intercession,
was left unaided.

Inspired by this confidence, I fly to you,
O Virgin of virgins, my Mother;
to you do I come, before you I stand,
sinful and sorrowful.

O Mother of the Word Incarnate,
despise not my petitions, but in your
mercy hear and answer me.
Amen.

HISTORY AND BACKGROUND

The *Memorare*, a prayer invoking the intercession of Mary, is often attributed to the twelfth-century Cistercian monk and abbot St. Bernard of Clairvaux, who had a great devotion to the Blessed Virgin. However, while some of his writings do echo the words of the *Memorare*, he did not compose it.

The text of the prayer that that we use today is a section of a much longer prayer known as the "*Ad sanctitatis tuae pedes, dulcissima Virgo Maria*" ("At your holy feet, most sweet Virgin Mary"). This prayer was composed in the fifteenth century, three hundred years after Saint Bernard's death. The actual author of the "*Ad sanctitatis tuae pedes, dulcissima Virgo Maria*" is unknown.

By the early sixteenth century, Catholics had begun to pray and use the *Memorare*—the short section of this longer prayer—as a separate prayer. St. Francis de Sales, bishop of Geneva in the early seventeenth century, was very devoted to the *Memorare*. Fr. Claude Bernard, a seventeenth-century French priest, a zealous advocate of the prayer, stated that he learned the prayer from his father. Fr. Bernard used it extensively in his ministry to the poor, to prisoners, and to criminals condemned to death. It is said that he had some 200,000 copies of the prayer printed and distributed in leaflets in various languages during his lifetime (a time before social media and the internet).

Father Bernard's promotion of the *Memorare* brought the prayer the popularity it enjoys today. It is believed that Father Bernard's name led to the confusion with, and false attribution of the prayer to, Saint Bernard of Clairvaux.

Today, Catholics pray the *Memorare* at various times; many have said that it is especially helpful for them during times of difficulty or distress. St. Teresa of Calcutta taught others to pray it when they most needed help. She herself often prayed it whenever she was faced with an emergency situation.

REFLECTING ON THE WORDS OF THE PRAYER

Remember,

"*Mom, remember when...*" How many times—when we wanted or needed something from our mothers (or fathers)—did we invite them to remember what they promised in the past, to remember what they did or said in the past, sometimes even offhandedly?

Even though we don't need to remind Mary to remember, we go to Mary with trusting confidence, just as we approach others in our lives who we know are intimately concerned about us and always available to listen, to care, and to help.

Even though Mary needs no reminder of her role in God's story, perhaps we are the ones who need reminders. We need to be reminded of our role in the communion of saints, of our interdependence with all of God's family, of our interconnectedness with Mary, whom Jesus gave to us as our mother too.

The first word of the prayer in Latin is *memorare*: "remember"... we begin this prayer, then, with a confident invitation to Mary, with a necessary reminder to ourselves.

O most gracious Virgin Mary,

As we call on Mary, we name her "gracious."

"Gracious" comes from the Latin word for good will. When we think of gracious people, we envision people of kindness, courtesy, generosity of spirit, and compassion. A gracious host places flowers in the room, leaves extra blankets, unique toiletries, and even (especially!) chocolates for overnight guests to enjoy. Even during a difficult moment—for instance, when a waiter spills coffee on your jacket—a gracious person remains thoughtful and kind.

Mary was probably gracious in these ways of kindness, thoughtfulness, and generosity. When we use the word in prayer, the meaning goes much deeper.

Psalm 67:1 says, "May God be gracious to us and bless us..." In the blessing in Numbers 6:25, we read, "May the Lord cause his face to shine upon you, and be gracious to you." Another definition of "gracious" is "to favor." God favors us, blesses us, and intimately shares God's very life—grace—with us. Mary is gracious because she is filled with God's life, grace.

The Catholic belief of Mary's graciousness—Mary's fullness of God's life, grace—is rooted in the greeting of the angel in Luke 1:28. Mary is spoken of as "full of grace," which in Greek means one who has been and continues to be "favored" or "graced" by God. In this gospel a new name is given to Mary: Favored One, one who is fully graced. Mary, from the first moment of her being, was graced. For the rest of her days she didn't just *know* God but continually grew in, and lived, a Godlike life.

A woman who longed to know about heaven prayed constantly, "O God, grant me in this life a vision of paradise." One night an angel came in a dream, leading her to heaven. They walked down a street in paradise until they came to an ordinary looking house. The angel, pointing toward the house said, "Go and look inside." The woman found a person preparing dinner, another reading the newspaper, and children playing with their toys. Disappointed, she said to the angel: "Is this all there is to heaven?" The angel replied, "Those people you saw in that house are not in paradise, paradise is in them!"

To the people of her neighborhood, Mary was a simple Jewish girl. The angel's message named her uniqueness: the Lord is with you; you are gracious; paradise is in you.

Mary lived her daily life—the small moments, the joys and sorrows, as well as the larger challenges—graciously, in a trusting relationship with God, continually aware of the presence of God, always and everywhere. This is one of the outstanding ways Mary is our model, our companion. The angel's foundational message is also a message to each of us: paradise is in you; the Lord is with you; you are graced.

that never was it known that anyone who fled to your protection, implored your help, or sought your intercession, was left unaided.

The sentence structure and some of these words might not be what we find in our usual, everyday conversations, yet they give us a very poetic prayer.

Let's explore some of the words:

- **Fled:** fled is usually used to mean run *away from* something, to escape, to bolt or abscond. Here it means the opposite: to run *to* Mary for safety, security, and shelter.
- **Implored:** implored is an intense word that connotes begging sincerely, urgently, or desperately. We implore when we ask someone in a determined, earnest, and sometimes emotional way to do or not to do something.
- **Intercession:** the word intercession is often used when speaking about prayer, about the role of Mary and the saints with us. Intercession means pleading on behalf of someone else. (Prayers of petition, expressing our awareness of our relationship with God, ask for the things we need—

primarily spiritual needs, but also physical ones as well. See the *Catechism of the Catholic Church*, 2629–2633.)

- **Unaided:** At times we might use this word with a positive focus: She was able to walk unaided after surgery. In our prayer, it conveys "without help" as well as "being left on one's own; abandoned."

Calling on Mary to remember that "never was it known..." might be seen as a bold act; but it is a boldness built on our needs and the reverence, confidence, and trust that Catholics have for Mary.

These words, however, do not lead us to regard this prayer as miraculous. They do not mean that the requests we make while praying the *Memorare* are automatically granted, or answered in the way we envision. As with any prayer, when we humbly ask Mary's help through the *Memorare*, we will always receive a response, but we might not recognize it at first; it may look very different from our desire.

Inspired by this confidence, I fly to you, O Virgin of virgins, my Mother; to you do I come, before you I stand, sinful and sorrowful.

No matter our age, we want to race (fly) to our moms (and dads) when we're sad and in trouble (and when good things have happened). Catholics, of course, can, and often do, pray directly to God. At the same time, the Second Vatican Council also recognized the "close and indissoluble tie" that unites Mary to her divine Son (*Lumen Gentium*, 53). Mary is intimately united to Jesus, and she is "our mother in the order of grace" (*Lumen Gentium*, 61).

When Jesus from the cross said to St. John, "Behold your Mother" (John 19:27), his mother became ours as well.

We pray again—in this line—with certainty, because Mary is our mother who deeply cares for us amid our faults and in our goodness, in our difficult times and in our joys.

O Mother of the Word Incarnate, despise not my petitions, but in your mercy hear and answer me. Amen.

Mary is our mother because she was, first, the Mother of the Word Incarnate, Jesus, the Word of God made flesh. Jesus became human through Mary. Mary cares for us because she is our mother and the mother of Jesus, who cares so much for us that he became one of us.

Mary, as the first disciple, lived as Jesus challenged us: "Be merciful, as your Father is merciful" (Luke 6:36). Because of Mary's loving kindness and compassion, we confidently pray that Mary will not discard or reject our prayers.

QUESTIONS FOR REFLECTION AND CONVERSATION

Remember—*What gospel stories about Mary do you most remember?*

Remember—*How/when has Mary been a part of your life?*

Remember—*What prayer(s) to Mary did you most often use in your childhood? What Marian prayer(s) do you use today?*

The following prayer, first found in a Greek papyrus, c. 300, is the oldest known prayer to Mary: "We fly to thy protection, O holy Mother of God. Despise not our petitions in our necessities, but deliver us always from all dangers, O glorious and blessed Virgin." How does this prayer compare to the **Memorare**? *Does it have the elements of other Marian prayers?*

IDEAS FOR CONTINUING PRAYER

- You might want to pray a shortened version of the prayer: "Remember, most loving Virgin Mary, never was it heard that anyone who turned to you for help was left unaided. Inspired by this confidence, though burdened by my faults and failings, I run to you for protection for you are my mother."
- With its brevity and simplicity, the *Memorare* can be easy to memorize. As you pray it often, let it become a part of your frequent prayer to Mary.
- For many people, praying in song helps memorizing and enables going deeper into the meaning of the words. There are various versions of the *Memorare* in song available; a few of them:
  https://www.youtube.com/watch?time_continue=6&v=H93HaDeg27c
  https://www.youtube.com/watch?v=EGZ_InZ-88o
  https://www.youtube.com/watch?v=QVXiFogEM-o
  https://www.youtube.com/watch?v=yjK8zXwp8ow
  https://www.youtube.com/watch?v=QyPdpBfGbyQ

https://www.youtube.com/watch?v=R_uPu7G-aVI
https://www.youtube.com/watch?v=H93HaDeg27c
There are also a number of videos available of the prayer itself (without music).

- Write your own prayer of confidence in Mary's care, requesting her intercession for your needs.
- Many people pray the *Memorare* when they are about to begin a trip in the car—whether it be a quick drive to the neighborhood store or a longer outing.

SUGGESTIONS FOR FAMILIES AND/OR CATECHETICAL SESSIONS

Watch "Mary in 2 Minutes" (https://www.youtube.com/watch?v=j7AQGyqtoKo&feature=youtu.be).

Plant a Marian garden: flowers (and sometimes herbs) whose names or forms are traditionally associated with Mary (https://www.franciscanmedia.org/honoring-mary-in-your-garden/ and https://www.catholicnewsagency.com/cw/post.php?id=502).

Explore and pray the Litany of Mary and its many titles for Mary.

The ANGELUS

V. The Angel of the Lord declared unto Mary,
R. And she conceived of the Holy Spirit.
Hail Mary, ...

V. Behold the handmaid of the Lord.
R. Be it done unto me according
to Your Word.
Hail Mary, ...

V. And the Word was made flesh,
R. And dwelt among us.
Hail Mary, ...

V. Pray for us, O holy Mother of God.

R. That we may be made worthy of the promises of Christ.

Let us pray:

Pour forth, we beseech You, O Lord,
Your Grace into our hearts;
that as we have known the incarnation of Christ, your Son
by the message of an angel,
so by His passion and cross
we may be brought to the glory of His Resurrection.
Through the same Christ, our Lord.
Amen.

HISTORY AND BACKGROUND

You might have seen the famous nineteenth-century painting by Jean-François Millet: *The Angelus*. This painting depicts the simplicity and the prevalence of the Angelus prayer for centuries. In this 1857 painting we see a farming couple in a potato field pausing at dusk to pray as they hear the *Angelus* bell. In 1865, Millet said: "The idea for *The Angelus* came to me because I remembered that my grandmother, hearing the church bell ringing while we were working in the fields, always made us stop work to say the Angelus prayer."

The *Angelus*—its name coming from the opening Latin words *Angelus Domini* (the angel of the Lord)—is prayed three times a day (6 am; noon; 6 pm) with three Biblical verses, alternating with the "Hail Mary." Because it is anchored with the three Hail Marys, it is seen as a Marian prayer. At the same time, its focus is on the important mystery of the Incarnation, God becoming one of us.

Many historians have slightly different versions of the origins of this spiritual practice. This devotion did not appear suddenly but developed over several centuries. It is generally thought to have begun at least seven hundred years ago. The monks and nuns of the Middle Ages were called to their regularly scheduled and structured prayer life by the ringing of bells. This call to prayer—throughout the day—was a constant reminder to pause in their daily lives to remember and praise God.

The monks and nuns prayed the Divine Office (Liturgy of the Hours). At a time when many of the faithful were illiterate, the *Angelus* allowed the laity to pray at set times throughout the day without needing to know how to read the Psalms.

The evening Angelus seems to have become the first practice. There was a tradition in the monasteries to ring a bell at dusk as they began evening prayer and as a kind of salute to the Virgin Mary. This was then embraced by the churches, where the faithful were encouraged to pray three Hail Marys in honor of the visit of the angel to Mary, which some believed to have occurred during the evening.

The morning Angelus grew from the practice of ringing a morning bell, honoring Mary as the "Morning Star" and the custom of praying three Hail Marys while this bell called the monks to the first prayer of the day.

The Angelus prayed at noon seems to be the last to develop. It probably had its origin in the ringing of a noon bell based on the long-standing practice of praying and meditating on Our Lord's passion at midday each Friday.

Today's form of the Angelus, with its antiphons, Hail Marys, and final prayer, came about in the sixteenth century and is found for the first time in a catechism printed in Venice in 1560.

In 1742, Pope Benedict XIV directed that the *Regina Caeli* (Queen of Heaven) be prayed instead of the *Angelus* during the Easter season. It is a prayer of rejoicing; we pray—with Mary—because we have been given new life through the resurrection.

The church, through various recent popes, has affirmed the importance of the *Angelus*. Since the time of St. John XXIII, the pope delivers an address every Sunday at noon, known as the *Angelus* address. At the end, the pope leads the praying of the *Angelus* (or *Regina Caeli*) and concludes with a blessing for those in Saint Peter's Square and those watching via television. In his apostolic letter *Marialis Cultus* (1974), Pope Paul VI indicated that the *Angelus* is an important reminder to Catholics of the Paschal Mystery, in which by recalling the incarnation of the Son of God they pray that they may be led "through his passion and cross to the glory of his resurrection" (41). Following the Synod of Bishops on the Word of God, Pope Benedict XVI wrote in *Verbum Domini* (2010): "The Synod also recommended that the faithful be encouraged to pray the Angelus. This prayer, simple yet profound, allows us to commemorate daily the mystery of the Incarnate Word. It is only right that the People of God, families and communities of consecrated persons, be faithful to this Marian prayer traditionally recited at sunrise, midday and sunset."

REFLECTING ON THE WORDS OF THE PRAYER

The Angel of the Lord declared unto Mary, and she conceived of the Holy Spirit.

Through the words of Luke (1:26–38) we hear how God entered human history. God entered Mary's history, and this reminds us that God is always asking, too, to enter *our* lives. Mary—as our model of discipleship—was the first to hear the Good News and welcome it. Through her faith in God's word that the angel proclaimed, she conceived Jesus, the Son of God. We, too, are invited to play a part in bringing Jesus to our world.

Behold the handmaid of the Lord. Be it done unto me according to Your Word.

We remember Mary's "yes." Referring to herself as God's handmaid, Mary replies that she was open to whatever God would ask of her.

We are invited to reflect on our life through the lens of Mary's response. How do we say yes when God calls us to respond to the requests for help from those we meet on our daily journeys? or to be charitable in irritating situations? or to bring God's forgiving love to others?

And the Word was made flesh, and dwelt among us.

In the third invocation, we meditate on the greatest event in human history—the coming of the Son of God to earth. Our prayer reminds us of God's constant and intimate presence with us; our God became one of us; we are never alone.

This invocation is not only a historic reminder of the Incarnation; it is also an invitation to live this mystery in our daily lives. We live the Incarnation when we are Christlike to all those in our daily lives. We live the Incarnation when we are the hands of Jesus to serve, comfort, and support those around us.

Pray for us, O holy Mother of God. That we may be made worthy of the promises of Christ.

This final invocation echoes the Hail Mary and the Rosary ("that meditating upon these mysteries of the most holy Rosary of the Blessed Virgin Mary, we may imitate what they contain and obtain what they promise").

We ask Mary's help to live our Christian vocation, our pilgrimage of faith.

Pour forth, we beseech You, O Lord, Your Grace into our hearts; that as we have known the incarnation of Christ, your Son by the message of an angel, so by his passion and cross we may be brought to the glory of his Resurrection. Through the same Christ, our Lord. Amen.

The closing prayer is a central reminder of God's immense love for us in sending his Son so that, by his passion and cross, we may be brought to the glory of his resurrection.

In *Verbum Domini* (2010), Pope Benedict XVI encouraged us: "In the *Angelus* we ask God to grant that, through Mary's intercession, we may imitate her in doing his will and in welcoming his word into our lives. This practice can help us to grow in an authentic love for the mystery of the incarnation" (#88).

QUESTIONS FOR REFLECTION AND CONVERSATION

The ***Angelus*** *is a prayer that continually—throughout the busy times of our day—calls us to be conscious of God's presence. What other practices do you have that call you to be aware of God with you during the hustle and bustle of everyday life?*

How does the reality of the Incarnation comfort you? challenge you?

IDEAS FOR CONTINUING PRAYER

- Set reminders in your phone for 6:00 a.m., noon, and 6:00 p.m. to remind you that it is time to pray the *Angelus* (or the *Regina Caeli* during the fifty days of Easter).
- Try using one of the apps, available for Android and iPhone, that help you pray the Angelus.
- The *Angelus* is especially appropriate during Advent, and its final week, which focuses on the life of Mary.

SUGGESTIONS FOR FAMILIES AND/OR CATECHETICAL SESSIONS

Make a pact with family members that, no matter where each person is at noon each day (work, home, school, shopping, etc.), they will stop to pray the *Angelus* or three Hail Marys.

For centuries, everyone prayed the *Angelus*: the laborers in the fields, the owners of the land, the monks, the kings and queens, etc. Everyone was one and equal—in prayer. As you pray the *Angelus*, reflect together on the unity of all humankind; let go of barriers and walls that are often constructed by our culture. Share ideas of how prayer can lead you to working for a world of unity and equality.

The MAGNIFICAT

My soul proclaims the greatness of the Lord,
my spirit rejoices in God my Savior;
for he has looked with favor on his lowly servant.

From this day all generations
   will call me blessed:
the Almighty has done great things for me,
and holy is his Name.

He has mercy on those who fear him
in every generation.

He has shown the strength of his arm,
he has scattered the proud in their conceit.

He has cast down the mighty from their thrones,
and has lifted up the lowly.

He has filled the hungry with good things,
and the rich he has sent away empty.

He has come to the help of his servant Israel
for he has remembered his promise of mercy,
the promise he made to our fathers,
to Abraham and his children forever.

HISTORY AND BACKGROUND

The *Magnificat*, known as the Canticle of Mary in the Liturgy of the Hours, is from Luke's gospel (1:46–55). After Mary greets her cousin Elizabeth, who is pregnant with John the Baptist, John moves within Elizabeth's womb. Elizabeth praises Mary for her faith, and Mary replies with her prayer of praise—her response to her surprising pregnancy and her extraordinary child. It is the longest set of words spoken by a woman in the New Testament.

Even though it is Mary's prayer, it's not about her. The emphasis of the prayer rests on God, the Mighty One of Israel. Every sentence, except for the first two, has God has its subject. In those first two, God is the one through whose generosity Mary finds herself blessed.

The *Magnificat* invites all of us to pray in praise of God. Praying this prayer, we pray with Mary to God. The *Catechism of the Catholic Church* describes the *Magnificat* as "the song both of the Mother of God and of the Church" (CCC, 2619). Pope Francis has said of the *Magnificat*: "It is the song of hope; it is the song of the People of God walking through history. It is the song of many saints, men and women, some famous, and very many others unknown to us but known to God: mums, dads, catechists, missionaries, priests, sisters, young people, even children and grandparents" (Homily, August 15, 2015). In the *Magnificat*, Mary speaks for herself, for her community, and for the people of God throughout time.

The *Magnificat* resonates with the Old Testament hymn of praise that Hannah (1 Samuel 2:1–10) sang to God for answering her prayer (to have a child) and for taking the side of the needy. Mary's *Magnificat* also foreshadows many themes that appear later in the Gospel of Luke and in the ministry of Jesus.

REFLECTING ON THE WORDS OF THE PRAYER

My soul proclaims the greatness of the Lord,
my spirit rejoices in God my Savior;
for he has looked with favor on his lowly servant.
From this day all generations will call me blessed:
the Almighty has done great things for me,
and holy is his Name.

Mary responds to Elizabeth's affirmation of her with these words. She mentions what God has done for her as an individual: looked on her with esteem, done great things, and given her a lasting reputation for holiness. Mary responds to these blessings by praising and magnifying God.

Some translations of Luke's gospel say: "My soul magnifies the Lord." The Greek word for "magnify" means to extol, glorify, make the greatness known, to deem or declare great, to esteem highly, to celebrate. Mary attributes nothing to herself. She knows that all that has happened to her is gift from the Almighty, the one whose very essence is greatness and compassion.

Mary never draws attention to herself but instead uses the gifts given her to reflect, to echo, God's greatness. Mary's *Magnificat*—and her very life—work to make God's glory more visible.

Many Scripture scholars have speculated on what constitutes Mary's lowliness. Is it her humility, her social position (she belongs to the poor of Luke's gospel), the degradation of the Jewish people at the time (especially suffered by women)? Whatever it is (and perhaps it is all of these), Mary rejoices that God views her lowliness with preferential eyes.

The ending words of this portion reconnect with the beginning of Mary's prayer: the very name of the Lord God our Savior is holy. The goodness, the holiness, the generosity of God is all-pervasive.

He has mercy on those who fear him
in every generation.

Mary is captivated by God's mercy. As a Jew, Mary knew that the very definition of God is mercy: "The Lord, the Lord, a God gracious and merciful, slow to anger, and abounding in love and fidelity" (Exodus 34:6).

Because of this conviction of God's mercy, fear does not mean fright or anxiety but a sense of profound awe, steadfast trust, and unwavering confidence.

God's mercy and blessing are not just for Mary or Elizabeth, or for the Jewish people of the time; they are for generation to generation: from now until the end of time.

He has shown the strength of his arm,
he has scattered the proud in their conceit.
He has cast down the mighty from their thrones,
and has lifted up the lowly.
He has filled the hungry with good things,
and the rich he has sent away empty.

Earlier, Mary proclaimed that God's name is holy. Now, Mary names the way holiness expresses itself. Some might believe that because God is great, God is partial to those who are great (in the eyes of the world), and that because God is exalted, God favors what is exalted among men and women. The opposite is true. God's holiness expresses itself by exalting the lowly and opposing the arrogant.

The *Magnificat* changes the order of things. Often our world is impressed with money, power, and status. Mary proclaims that God reverses the usual way of viewing the world; God's vision and care turn everything upside down. Mary praises God for promising to be present to the humble, the poor, and those on the margins.

In her prayer, Mary not only announces a birth, she names the beginning of a new world, one very different from any social order that relies on oppression, power, and exploitation to achieve greatness. Because this is so crucial, Mary mentions it three times, stressing that it isn't just about compassionate *feelings*, but it is lived in concrete saving actions for those who are outcast and suffering.

The *Magnificat* contains echoes of many of Jesus' messages and concerns, especially in the Beatitudes where all those who are humble, pure of heart, full of mercy, and willing to grieve and suffer persecution to bring peace and justice to the world are called blessed, favored, and fortunate

He has come to the help of his servant Israel
for he has remembered his promise of mercy,
the promise he made to our fathers,
to Abraham and his children forever.

Mary ends her song of praise by focusing on Israel, God's people, and Abraham, the father in faith of all God's people. Mary understands the compassion shown to her as typical of how God has responded to God's covenant people. Mary's canticle links together the whole story of Israel throughout the ages, grounded in God's loyal love and faithfulness to promises. Mary knows that she—and God's people—will always experience the presence of God's protection, strength, and nurture.

QUESTIONS FOR REFLECTION AND CONVERSATION

*Does the **Magnificat** cause you to see Mary in a new way?*

*What words in the **Magnificat** comfort you? challenge you?*

In Mary's prayer, the lowly are raised up, the hungry are filled, and the proud are scattered in their conceit. What does this mean in our day and age?

IDEAS FOR CONTINUING PRAYER

- Mary's hymn is not an exact duplicate of Hannah's words. Rather, it seems that Mary was so steeped in Scripture that when she responds to Elizabeth's greeting, the words that come to her are the words of Scripture. Pope Benedict XVI spoke about "Mary's familiarity with the word of God. This is clearly evident in the *Magnificat*. There we see in some sense how she identifies with the word, enters into it;...The *Magnificat*...is entirely woven from threads of Holy Scripture.... we see how completely at home Mary is with the word of God, with ease she moves in and out of it. She speaks and thinks with the word of God" (*Verbum Domini*, 28). Include reflection on Scripture in your daily prayer so that your minds and hearts are guided by God's word as easily as Mary's were.

- Pray the *Magnificat*, rephrasing and adapting the words to your own life—and the life of our world—right now.
- The *Magnificat* provides reflection on the Visitation, the second Joyful Mystery of the Rosary. Pray the Joyful mysteries of the Rosary with the words of the *Magnificat* as a backdrop.
- There are many musical settings of the *Magnificat* (Palestrina, Bach, Mozart, and various contemporary ones). Using YouTube or other sources, pray the *Magnificat* in song.

SUGGESTIONS FOR FAMILIES AND/OR CATECHETICAL SESSIONS

Create a litany about the promises God has made and kept throughout the history of God's people; include the promises God has made and kept for your life together during this time.

Make a large mural that illustrates, "the Almighty has done great things for me."

Pray the *Magnificat* as you end each day.

ACTS *of* FAITH, HOPE, *and* LOVE

ACT OF FAITH

O my God, I firmly believe
that you are one God in three divine Persons,
Father, Son, and Holy Spirit.
I believe that your divine Son became man
and died for our sins and that he will come
to judge the living and the dead.
I believe these and all the truths
which the Holy Catholic Church teaches
because you have revealed them
who are eternal truth and wisdom,
who can neither deceive nor be deceived.
In this faith I intend to live and die.
Amen.

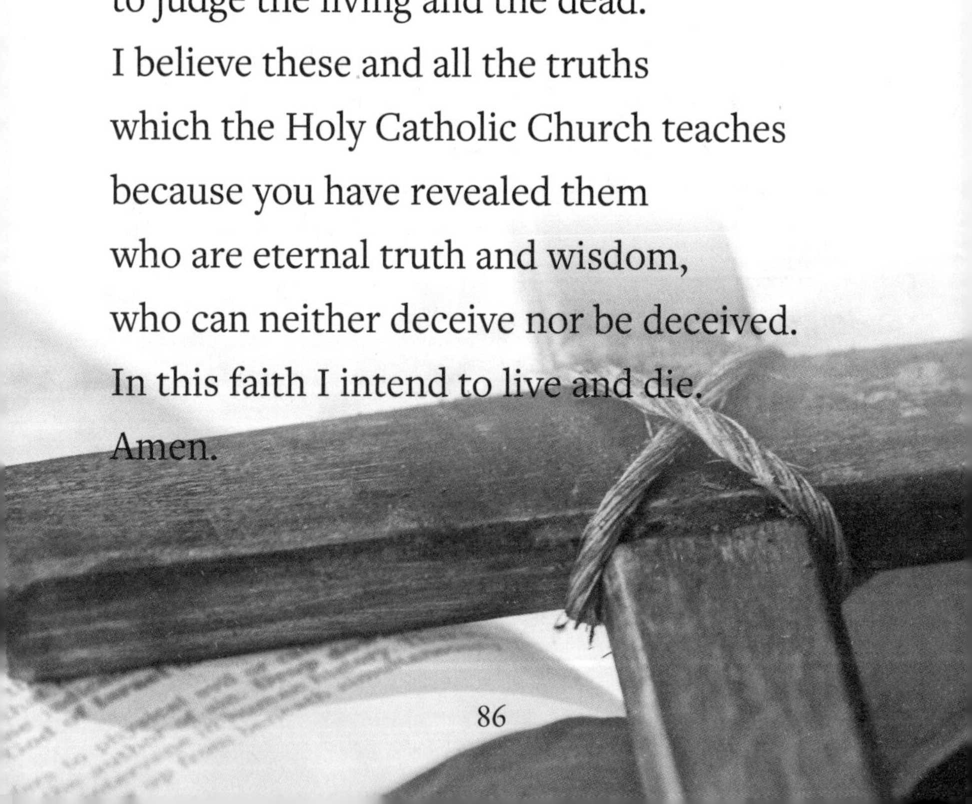

ACT OF HOPE

O Lord God, I hope by your grace
for the pardon of all my sins
and after life here to gain eternal happiness
because you have promised it
who are infinitely powerful, faithful, kind,
and merciful.
In this hope I intend to live and die.
Amen.

ACT OF LOVE

O Lord God, I love you above all things
and I love my neighbor for your sake
because you are the highest, infinite
and perfect good,
worthy of all my love.
In this love I intend to live and die.
Amen.

HISTORY AND BACKGROUND

In his letter to the Corinthians St. Paul wrote: "So faith, hope, and love remain, these three; but the greatest of these is love" (1 Corinthians 13:13). In our baptism we are gifted with three theological virtues and the seven gifts of the Holy Spirit. The three theological (which means belonging to or relating to God) virtues are: faith, hope, and love; they have God as their foundation; they root our lives in God as the core purpose and motivation of all we do. These virtues empower us to deepen our relationship with God, to vibrantly live our relationship with all those in God's family.

As with any gift, we are called to use these virtues, to develop them, to grow in them. If we ignore them and they lay dormant, we ignore God's gift. As the *General Directory for Catechesis* reminds us, "Faith is a gift destined to grow in the hearts of believers" (56). We cooperate with God; we are called to be active in the growth of faith (and hope and love).

We grow in faith, hope, and love through our continual actions and our prayer. The apostles said to the Lord, "Increase our faith" (Luke 17:5). Thus, the church, over the years, has recommended that we pray acts of faith, hope, and love each morning. Rowan Williams, the retired archbishop of Canterbury, in a 2010 address, said, "In the Christian life, faith is what happens to our understanding; hope is what happens to our remembering; and love is what happens to our wanting. To grow up as a Christian is to take that journey from understanding into faith, from memory into hope and from will into love" (http://www.abc.net.au/religion/faith-hope-and-charity-in-the-world-today/10102038).

Throughout the years, and today, different wordings are often found in various collections of prayers. The wording of the prayers given here can be found in the *Compendium of the Catechism of the Catholic Church*.

REFLECTING ON THE WORDS OF THE PRAYER

The Act of Faith

The Act of Faith is basically a summary of the Apostles Creed and asserts the mystery of faith that we proclaim at Mass: Christ's death, resurrection, and second coming.

One of the dimensions of faith is that it is belief in a truth on the word of another, though that truth might not be fully understood. In this prayer, we give the reason why we believe: God has revealed the truths. Even though, at times, we might not understand, we believe because God, who is wisdom and truth, has guided the church in these beliefs and teachings.

Embedded in this Act of Faith is another dimension of the reality of faith: faith is a dependable relationship, not only belief in a list of dogma and doctrines. Our confidence is rooted in the reality of God, in the reality that God has first reached out to us in relationship. Faith is a journey of deepening intimacy.

The Act of Hope

The Act of Hope is a confident prayer of our firm trust in God who is always faithful. In hopeful trust, we know that God is, and always will be, with us, guiding us to live so that we will be with God forever.

Hope is the driving force of all human initiative, a central theme in Scripture, and the only way to live a life of discipleship. Optimism says: "keep hoping; things will get better. Christian hope is more realistic: "Things may well get worse, anything may happen, but God is on our side."

The Act of Love

In heaven, faith and hope will not be needed: we will already know; we will already possess what we have hoped for. But love is everlasting; the love we lived on earth—for God and others—will continue to deepen.

The Act of Love—prayed often—opens our heart to living a love that is more than simply "doing good." The two great commandments (loving God and our neighbor as ourselves) call us to an unconditional, life-encompassing, community-impacting commitment to God and a willingness to place the needs, happiness, and well-being of others above our own.

QUESTIONS FOR REFLECTION AND CONVERSATION

Reflecting on the Act of Faith, what do you believe about God, Jesus, and the Holy Spirit? What truths of our faith have comforted you? challenged you?

Reflecting on the Act of Hope, what do you look forward to because of your relationship with God?

Reflecting on the Act of Love, why do you love God? For what are you grateful? When do you find it easy (and difficult) to love others?

IDEAS FOR CONTINUING PRAYER

- Throughout the day, pray simply: "Jesus, I believe in you. Jesus, I hope in you. Jesus, I love you." (Sometimes you might pray to God the Father; at other times, to the Holy Spirit.)

- Using your own words, write an act of faith, an act of hope, and an act of love.

- During one week (or month) concentrate on praying for a deepening of faith; after that time, focus on hope, and then on love. Pray each morning; in the evening reflect on how you lived that virtue that day.

SUGGESTIONS FOR FAMILIES AND/OR CATECHETICAL SESSIONS

Send greeting cards—or email messages—to people you know who could use a note of faith, hope, or love.

Painting rocks and leaving them in places for people to find has become a popular practice. Paint rocks with messages of faith, hope, and love, leaving them in various places throughout your neighborhood.

Explore some of the symbols that the church has used for faith (cross), hope (anchor), and love (heart). Design some additional symbols.

What if we talked about "services of love/charity" rather than service projects?